New Thinking in Public Art:

Habitat

Environment

Community

ISBN 1 873352 34 4

public works **:** **If you can't find it,**
give us a ring

Working with uncertainty towards
a real public space

Doina Petrescu

ARTicle Press Publishers & ixia PA Ltd

CONTENT

Foreword
Anna Douglas

Interview
public works + John Butler & Janet Hodgson

Project:
If you can't find it, give us a ring
public works

Essay:
Working with uncertainty towards a real public space.
Doina Petrescu

Foreword

The *New Thinking in Public Art* series, initiated by ixia, the UK's public art think tank, explores the increased integration of artists into regeneration practices. Artists have for many years contributed to urban renewal. They have done so primarily in two ways: creating memorials and landmarks — all be it eschewing the tradition of figurative statuary — and by contributing aesthetic and practical solutions as part of multi- disciplinary design teams. Transforming unloved and worn out spaces into places with identity has become one of the core functions of public art and has, arguably, defined the role of the 'public art artist'.

However, responding to current artistic and architectural practices, ixia wants to open up fresh thinking on defining 'public art' and the role of artists within public realm development. With each volume in this three part series — habitat, community and environment — an artist or group, for whom working within the public arena provides the context for their work, has been commissioned to produce a new *art project*. This approach may be perplexing for readers looking for models for artistic intervention, but this publication is not intended to offer case studies; instead, we present art as a means to introduce ideas that are relevant to all those working in public realm development right now.

In addition, each book includes an *interview* with the artist and a commissioned *essay* by a leading commentator on architecture or urban regeneration, which draws on themes implied by the artist project, and, like a supporting bridge, carries these into the professional fields of urban development.

We are grateful to **public works** for accepting the challenge of contributing to this publication a new spatial reading and illustration of their project *Park Products* (initially commissioned by Serpentine Gallery), and to Doina Petrescu for her essay *'Working with uncertainty towards a real public space'*, which revisits the notions of *community, public* and *participation*. This mix of art and polemic we regard, in itself, as a new form of 'doing public art'.

Anna Douglas
Series Editor

INTERVIEW

Kathrin Böhm + Andreas Lang,

with John Butler & Janet Hodgson

Kathrin Böhm + Andreas Lang, of public works, with John Butler and Janet Hodgson

John Butler and Janet Hodgson met Kathrin Böhm and Andreas Lang, of **public works**, in their studio on December 5th 2005. The interview discussed three of their projects, *Mobile Porch, Lay-out Gasworks, and Makeshift Johannesburg.*

public works' conceptual interest lies in the relationship between institutions who govern public space and the users of those spaces. public works' practice consists of implementing communication structures and physical structures that support and make use of existing local networks and resources, and at the same time offer, propose and stimulate new programmes and built structures.

Mobile Porch, Westway fly-over, London

JH: How did the collaborative practice of public works evolve?

AL: *Mobile Porch was our first project. This set the basis for our future practice and our interest in 'one-to-one' activities and the informality of public spaces.*

KB: *Formerly, Stefan and I developed an art practice which was a lot about acting on site and demonstrating change, and involving an audience in changing spaces. That idea strongly influenced the brief for* **Mobile Porch***: to create a space for the urban context, where we could stage ad-hoc activities.*

AL: *We work with the notion that the* **Mobile Porch** *is a tool that can simultaneously address a large-scale situation and 'one-to-one' situations. From the beginning we felt confident that the Mobile Porch could help North Kensington Amenity Trust, who govern the land where the project took place, to think about their public spaces and their relationship with the public. For us, the term 'Mobile Porch' does not exclusively address the object. It is the marriage between the ad-hoc activities and the designed physical object.*

KB: *The **Mobile Porch** was on site for two months, always accompanied by one of us. We animated it simply by hanging out and offering it as a platform for whoever wanted to use it. We used the fact that the Mobile Porch was something strange looking to create curiosity, and curiosity is the first step towards a conversation with the public.*

AL: *We were clear we did not want people to use it commercially or politically.*

KB: *And, we would not have allowed extremist parties to use it to publish their views.*

JH: Is there an issue of *control* in that position?

KB: *The word 'control' suggests a feeling of superstition and doubt towards something. And it implies the wish to be in control of something. We never had a situation where there was a need for us to impose control. In our work, we establish infrastructures that allow for social situations which then, very often, drive themselves. Architectural*

Mobile Porch is used by a local poets group to launch their latest publication and do a public reading.

*theorist Jane Rendell called her essay for our **Park Products** 'Letting Go'; and I think this describes our approach very well.*

AL: *People hold a lot of assumptions about public spaces, and what might or might not happen. It is important to continually challenge these assumptions, and this is why we think it is important to let our projects run their life. Experience shows, that things do not always run out of control, that the reality (of a situation) is always different from what you anticipate. That realisation is of great value (to us).*

JB: So what was the *Mobile Porch*'s public usage? Was it local or generated through the art press?

KB: *It was mainly local. I think we had about forty, quite low key, ad-hoc events initiated by people who lived there or worked there. But, equally important, we had a very long list of things that could have happened;*

ideas that people developed or spontaneously came up with when being confronted with the **Mobile Porch**.

AL: *One key observation generated through the project, is that there is a strong need for non-commercial space and a need for space within the public realm that surprises you or encourages you.* **Mobile Porch** *revealed the lack of available non-commercial public platforms, and this was quite important for the Trust to understand. But to what degree they acted on this, we don't know. The organisation approached us one year later to talk about bringing the Porch back. They realised, however, when we went into negotiation, how much effort and commitment it takes to create an informal public space like that.*

KB: *Initially, after the project, we proposed that maybe, instead of an object, the Trust might hire someone to look after the informality of their social spaces, in the same way that the Trust employs a gardener who looks after the green public spaces. In that sense, our projects are*

Lay-out Gasworks, London; brainstorm session called 'Platform 02', as part of the open office on site.

prototypes, that test relationships through implementing temporary structures, both physical and conceptual structures.

AL: *We discussed why we needed such an expensive and sophisticated object as the Porch. Why couldn't we just use a cardboard box and invite people to play music? However, we do have a clear interest in designing things, in design language and the actual physical presence of objects* on site. At the time, it looked like a contradiction, between something socially engaged and something of a formal concern. But this is exactly the contradiction or conflict we are interested in; the relationship between informal social structures in the shaping of their physical environment.

JH: Did you ever record the mix of people that used the *Mobile Porch*?

AL: *It was with the **Lay-out** project for Gasworks Gallery that we started to record and instrumentalise the information encounters which happened during the on-site phase of the project; in order to develop a series of proposals, both architectural and programmatic ones. **Lay-out** started its Phase 1 in summer 2002 with Phase 2 in 2004. We were commissioned as an art and architectural team by Fiona Boundy, gallery curator, to develop a process that would allow Gasworks to understand their local potential as a cultural organisation.*

KB: *For two months we spent maybe three days a week on site, in what we called the open office. We simply opened the large shutter, which linked the gallery to the street, and moved in with our tables and chairs. The residency was like a series of spontaneous social events. It involved a lot of meeting and chatting to people who walked past from Tesco, and we invited other local institutions, organisations like the local authorities, theatres and other cultural partners. We also had brainstorming sessions with people involved in art and architectural activities.*

AL: *The **Open Office** established a direct and visible link to the street, and therefore to the general public. In addition, we started to use the façade as a way of demonstrating the activity by putting up posters. Over the two months, the façade became a document of our time there, and the different activities in and around Gasworks.*

KB: *Again, it is about hanging out and people being curious about why you are sitting in the street, and that is why you start having conversations. What was new with this project was that we established a website (www.gasworks.org.uk/layout) to archive all the different encounters, creating a database that has a search engine to find different categories. We archived them in a non-hierarchical order. What was important about **Lay-out**, as with **Mobile Porch**, was that every encounter was almost a proposal, or you could interpret every encounter as a proposal towards the public space of Gasworks. The website documents the encounter, but it also allowed us to very quickly record the ad-hoc proposals.*

JH: You describe your practice as having two elements, the objects and the encounters, both equally important. You don't describe the encounters, is there a reason why?

AL: *Though we often use anecdotes or quotes to represent the encounters, ultimately I guest one can't reconstruct the initial 'one-to-one' experience for a secondary audience. We give huge importance to the 'one-to-one'. At the same time, we can regard the pool of 'one-to-ones' as the resource for proposal for a further stage. The proposals address different issues, architectural ones, but also others, like the politics of regeneration.*

JB: How do you evaluate the impact of what you do? Is it purely cause and effect or is it literally that you observe, you stop at certain points and then pull away?

AL: *We don't hand over and withdraw. We hand over and say, 'this is what we think is a good idea', and allow the process to continue.*

JH: So how do you chose the ones that are a good idea?

KB: *The proposals derive from the overlaps in issues and interests which become visible during the on-site phase of the project. The proposals can be of a very different nature and scale, and some can be implemented by us. For instance, if the final project is an architectural one, we can provide that service quite easily.*

JB: How are the networks and different communities participating in these projects involved in the evaluation process?

AL: *We try to involve them, but that is a project in itself. This is what we are trying to do in this publication, by re-visiting **Park Products**. In the case of **Lay-out**, we were quite clear that we became the authors of the proposals. However, through the website it was easy to reference them back to the different encounters they originated from.*

JB: Are you the *authors* or the *transcribers*?

KB: *Yes, transcribers is actually a better term. It could be interesting to play with what we call ourselves. Ultimately, I don't think there is a compre-hensive term. I think that is something we are quite aware of, that we are handling something very informal, but we are formalising it too. We are either formalising it through turning it into proposals, or turning it into architecture, or turning it into objects like the **Mobile Porch**.*

JB: This relationship, between everyone who takes part in one of your projects, is important. Whilst you might be the authors, aren't the ideas the participant's, are they not *their* proposals?

KB: *You can probably call us the authors of the infrastructures that are set for each project - which instigate activity-based responses, and which we transcribe but also conclude and evaluate - as we're not mechanically collecting and recording responses. We're interested in the propositional quality of the responses and their translation into proposals which we pass on. We are not only entering informal networks within our projects, we are always part of a formalised relationship and try to transfer information from the informal side to the formal one. It's almost never about individual ideas, but about overlaps of ideas which we try to conclude.*

JH: With *Lay-out,* did you direct the conversations in the informal encounters, as you did in the brain storming session with the invited participants?

KB: *The informal encounters on site normally start with people asking us questions, rather than with us asking them questions. We tried to find out where they were from, why they'd stopped or if they already knew the space, but we didn't have a tick list. The encounters were representative of what happens there on a daily basis. Like, who walks past, who doesn't, who stops, who doesn't.*

JB: So is the *process* more or less important than the *outcome*?

AL: *The process is deliberately open and allows a lot of voices to guide and shape the outcome. The process sets the criteria by which any outcome or manifestation should be evaluated. I am interested to see to what degree the final outcome has the process embedded into it. This conclusion is an important moment of learning for any future projects. In the summer of 2005 in Johannesburg, South Africa, we worked at the* **The Bag Factory***, which is the sister gallery to Gasworks Gallery, and part of the same Triangle Arts Trust network. We were addressing the same question as we did with* **Lay-out***, of 'what is the local potential'? And the process was similar, but here we started to curate more events and we really appreciated the informality of this institution; the looseness of it. We wanted to understand it, so we talked to everyone in the building and tried to understand how they became part of it. To illustrate these stories we developed this* **iconic language** *and made* **narrative drawings** *that showed which circumstances nurtured the networks, a well as the relevant spaces in which the network actually took place.*

KB: *With the storylines, we were trying to record where people met and how it progressed into an engagement with the organisation. You don't have to become a member, you are assigned to an idea or your meet someone, therefore, you become part of a network. It was a snapshot, like whoever was there at the time.*

AL: *We were interested in why this community existed, where it was located and in what kind of physical building.*

The brainstorm session "Platform 02" is recorded and evaluated as part of the project related online database.

We tried to map out how much of what was actually taking place was at the Bag Factory itself.

JH: Have these drawings helped both you and Triangle Arts Trust understand and evaluate the network?

KB: *The drawings were for us to understand, at the time, but we also left the Trust a whole set of tools: maps, models, the flag and drawing systems, so that they could start considering which elements were important to them, in order to develop their organisation. The mapping is there for them to think about what to keep and what not to keep. We are trying to map activities that seem random to those who are part of the activity, but which might be of big relevance to the communal interest. It's often individually driven activities which are not considered as important with regard to the community, but, in fact, usually are. I will give an example. Through the mapping, we found out that a lot of artists undertake informal mentoring of students. They have established an educational programme over the years, but because it is so informal it wouldn't be called an education project, as such. Now, the Trust wants an educational space for a formalised education programme. Our recommendation was that they maintain the already successful informal education process, rather than implementing a formal one.*

JH: Can you talk about how your process differs from normal architectural practice?

AL: *I don't think many architectural practices immerse themselves to such a degree in the site, they work with a much more abstract and distant understanding of a site. If there is site engagement, it is often at the very beginning of a project, in the form of mapping or reading. Rarely is the*

Brainstorm session with Bag Factory artists on the different formal and informal programmes existing within their building

architectural process set up as a continuous exchange with the site and its users.

JB: Do you want to instigate social change through your practice and/ or play with your own roles? Are you responding to a market or working to commission in this process?

AL: *We want to outline alternatives. To do so sometimes means to play with different roles.*

KB: *I think partly it's because we do have different roles, (to Andreas). You are an architect, and I am an artist. But we swap or play with those roles because we want to. It is not necessarily the roles we give ourselves that we play with, but those given to us. I think a lot about the perception people have of us, and that is what we play with. So, if the public expect an architect to deliver a plan for a new building, then we don't do that. And we would almost use the fact that I am an artist to subvert their perception of what we might do. A lot of what we do is a subversive process.*

JH: What would you say is the historical or cultural context for your practice, both as art and architecture?

AL: *People like Cedric Price or Bernard Tschumi, people working at the AA (Architectural Association, London) in the 60s and 70s are important for us.*

KB: *I think historically, a certain intention to open up architecture towards participation probably happened at exactly the same time as in art.*

JH: And what is the specific notion of site in your work. You identify a site not as a place, but as a network of people, that you happen upon or bring together. You talk about the networks using a language that is normally used to describe permanent places and built architecture. Your use of language crosses over the two disciplines.

AL: *The other way to look at this might be to view architecture as a process, rather than as a product.*

KB: *And, I think we are trying to describe our process as a space. We are trying to place an architectural term onto something that is normally considered temporary, in flux, or informative. When you start looking at all these projects, it becomes clear that the spaces that are generated, even over a short period, can quite easily be looked at as sites. They can be described through their special make-up, and that is what starts interesting us. We perhaps would like a better answer to this, but that is definitely where our interests lie. To claim these networks as sites.*

JB: Is this what the architectural theorist Doina Petrescu has termed 'design action' the idea that you bring other interventions into the process; relational networks that form social architecture?

KB: *There is currently a more established debate about* social engagement *in art practice than there is in architectural practice.*

AL: *In architecture, social engagement mainly exists under the limited heading of consultation. However, a new debate in architecture does seem to be emerging, again—like what is happening at Sheffield University—but, it is very much in that laboratory phase within academia. There are very few live projects that really trust that* participatory process *enough to really inform the design, or the architecture.*

KB: *Or define themselves through the participative process. Whereas our art practice defines itself very much through* participation.

JB: Your practice provokes a generative process, doesn't it?, a spontaneous process of networking. There is direct public intervention and collaboration, facilitating individual expression and 'active goodwill', but is it democratically representative?

KB: *We're not choreographing a process, but setting structures which allow for a process to take shape and place. We sometimes describe our projects as publicising tools, for individual expression, which become relevant as events as such, but also as a snapshot of happening public life, as distinct from regulated public life.*

JB: You make a lot of interventions. Can you describe what informs the critical role for evaluating your projects, and how do the outcomes inform the development of your new work?

AL: *It's not a formal process. It happens at the beginning of each new project, in some way.*

KB: *We always look at the experience of the former project and what we valued most and how to extend those aspects into the next project.*

JB: Do you involve the networks and the different communities participating in these projects in the evaluation process?

AL: *We try, but evaluation is a project in itself. This is what we are trying to do in this publication be re-visiting* **Park Projects***.*

JH: You have described yourselves as neutral or apolitical in the way you work, is that a possible position?

KB: *Our practice is of course political. By 'apolitical', we mean we don't take sides when we step into a public project. We would never, for example, sit in front of Gasworks and say, we are pro something or anti it. This would block access to what we are trying to do.*

AL: *I think a lot of (our) projects depend on the generosity of people; that everyone enjoys contributing. This idea is built on the premise that if you are open, people are actually very happy to contribute and to share. I think that is a very precious space and we want people to respect it.*

JH: The public space is a contested area. How do you deal with conflict or differences. And how is this represented in your processes?

KB: *We try to keep our processes and debates transparent, that often resolves polarising conflict. Conflict is something you don't actually want, but, in fact, our work is about conflict. It is almost about pointing out the conflict and acknowledging it, approaching a process of constructively dealing with it, involving very different and at times opposing interests, and if possible agreeing on it.*

JH: Do you see your job as resolving conflicts or documenting them?

JB: ... and, do you think your *diagrammatic process* allows for the resolving of conflicts or their documentation?

Storyline mapping the access of one of the Bag Factory ar

AL: *I think the **diagrammatic process** allows us to gain a better understanding of those dynamics and conflicts. Architects often work with mappings to help their thinking and to help reach a conclusion, but it is an abstraction that the architect uses and that is also the problem. Our mapping processes are still at* an early stage of development. However, I agree with you, that it should stay accessible, to everyone, so that it becomes a language which tries to map the territories, or the qualities, or the networks we are interested in. Although text appears easy to understand, it nevertheless is still quite difficult to actually get into it. Our use of icons and diagrams is another attempt to visualise and explore those spaces under consideration more directly. And, it is more spatial than the *Lay-out* website, which maps narratives, but mainly relies on text to do so.

JB: I am wondering if this places the emphasis on the process, rather than the outcome. If you alone define the outcome you will have 'disruptive' conflicts; whereas, if you create a process of 'direct democracy' you and whoever else is involved in the project have to be of equal voice. Therefore, you can have conflict and differences. So, it seems that the process you work with is really important, rather, perhaps, than what you try to create?

AL: *If you encounter conflict in an art project you make a topic of this within the process. But if we are employed to deliver an access study, we have limited time and a different purpose, and therefore have to negotiate conflict in a different way.*

the network, and his activities within the building.

JH: Because you are commissioned, by a client, does that not, perhaps, position you as being employed by the very people who want an outcome?

KB: *Funnily enough, people hardly every identify us with the commissioning body. I think it has to do with how we appear on site.*

JB: Do they not identify you as 'experts'; either experts as architects or experts as artists?

KB: *We hang out on site and people just decide for themselves whether we have authority or not; how they want to see us.*

AL: *I think we appear as people who have an interest. And, that is the position we put forward first and formerly. And that open the discussion.*

Park Products stall, Kensington Gardens, August 2004.Commissioned by the Serpentine Gallery, London.

public works is a London-based art/architecture collective founded by architects Sandra Denicke-Polcher, Torange Khonsari, Andreas Lang and artists Kathrin Bohm and Stefan Saffe, who have been collaborating in different constellations since 1998.

**If you can't find it,
give us a ring.**

public works

graphic layout by public works

Park Products

Users of a public space

+

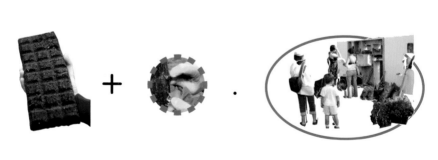

Its natural, social and cultural resources

⇓

Tradable items + Alternative currency . Market Place

A space

If you can't find it, give us a ring is a reoccurring quote from Park Products, a project commissioned by the Serpentine Gallery, which took place in and around Kensington Gardens, London, between September 2003 and October 2004.

The principle of Park Products is based on the idea of an informal economy as a generator for a new social space. The project linked people who work in Kensington Gardens and those who use the park for leisure with product design professionals to create a new range of tradable items These products make use of the park as a natural, cultural and social resource. The products wer later exchanged on a non-monetary basis with the general public of Kensington Gardens, using a mobile display and market stall.

If you can't find it, give us a ring refers to many of the spaces we have been using during the whole project, from hidden garden sheds to tucked away offices and private flats to the roaming stall.

If you can't find it, give us a ring also refers to Park Products as a complex spatial construct, which is spread across sites, time and memories. The Park Products space has its own particular social and physical qualities. It consists of existing spaces that we opened up, the adaptation of spaces and the new spaces that have been generated through the project.

This publication starts to draw Park Products as a space, by describing and outlining its different spatial components and scenarios. This description and acknowledgement is important to us in regards to a wider discussion about the shaping of public space.
Park Products created a space. That's our claim, and *If you can't find it, give us a ring.* *

public works

29

* The public works phone number is ++44. 20. 70 92 91 00

From space to space

Jim Rokos, product design student and former art support teacher at College Park School
Meeting at his studio at Central St. Martins College of Art & Design, 24/01/2006

"I took a friend rowing on the Serpentine Lake one day, and the boating guy told us that if I get a membership for the Royal Parks, it would be much cheaper the next time I went rowing. So I became a member and they kept sending me all this stuff. And one day there was some information about Park Products, and I thought, that looks interesting and got in contact. I met you guys and you described the project to me, but it wasn't clear to me what it was all about in the beginning. It seemed quite abstract.

It was great that we went to all those different areas in the park. Places where you normally don't have access to.

It was interesting how the different communities got involved. How for instance the classroom at our school became part of the premises for Park Products.

And of course Park Products created spaces in our head, where possibilities didn't become real, but still, they were existing, not part of the tangible world but part of our imagination. This space happened and might be left in our memory, or might get lost."

Jumping Rabbit Device in use

The Sackler Centre of Arts Education Space outdoor area.

Workshop with Year 9 students in their art space and later on in Kensington Gardens

Park College School in
Bayswater

testing of viewing
devices with students

At the time, Jim was working as a support teacher at College Park School in Bayswater.
We brainstormed a number of ideas for a new product, sitting on the lawn in front of the Education Space.
Later on we arranged for a visit to College Park School which lead to a number of workshops both at the school and in Kensington Gardens. The Park Re-view range was the outcome of those workshops and available at the Park Products stall.
Jim himself developed the Jumping Rabbit Device which enables visitors to see the Park through the eyes of a leaping rabbit, and which became the most popular item on the Park Products stall.

Kensington
Gardens Depot

31

Design studio

Kensington Gardens has a team of approximately twenty four gardeners, which are split into three groups: the Magazine group, the Flower walk group and the Kensington Palace group.

At the beginning of the project, the Magazine group met with Roger and Lynn from the Royal College of Art to have conversations about the park - their daily and seasonal work, and what they think is special about Kensington Gardens. Later on the various resources provided by the park were brainstormed, and initial prototypes for the Chompost Bar and the Fence Tools were discussed and tested.

Lynn Kingelin, product designer, former
Meeting at the Architectural Association

32

Meeting between Lynn and Roger Arquer from the Design Products MA at the Royal College of Arts and gardeners at the Magazine's canteen.

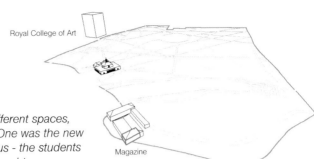

Royal College of Art

Magazine

" I guess the project was many different spaces, some more obvious than others. One was the new social space created by bringing us - the students - to the gardeners. The project brought so many aspects of the park as a space to light... like the compost pile, or the gardeners' sheds. It made us aware of the spaces. It was less about a visible or physical space, and more about designated social spaces, areas which overlap, and which could be superimposed as one network. The key thing was that people felt comfortable with it, to get involved, take their own time, on their own terms."

"Park Products for me was the bringing together of people who otherwise wouldn't come together like this. I wouldn't sit together with my team discussing aspects like design, etc. Normally it's all about money. It was about good will and kindship, people's good will. Basically giving good will to others."

Bennie Connolly, Sodexho Land Technology
Meeting at his office at the Magazine,
Kensington Gardens, 23/01/2006

33

Stories and places

The Kensington Palace gardeners group is in charge of keeping the area litter free.

On a regular basis they come across presents left for Prince William at the gate to Kensington Palace. They are left by a young woman who believes that she is William's mother. She brings letters, home cooked food, knitted baby clothes and collaged photographs of her and him. The gardeners have never seen the woman.

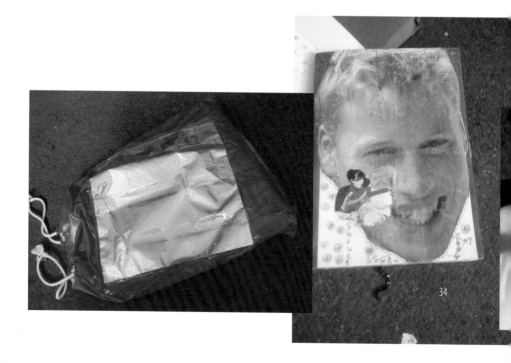

34

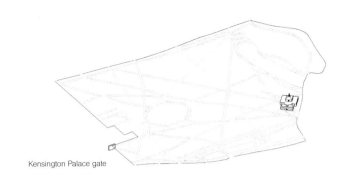

Kensington Palace gate

35

Space of interaction

The Flower Walk is a popular place, for visitors to the park and squirrels living in the park. Visitors love to feed the squirrels with peanuts, whereas the gardeners have an ongoing battle with the damage caused by those cute little animals.

Through conversations with the Flower Walk gardeners group, Tomek came up with the idea of a Squirrel Fun Toy, which allows playful interaction with the squirrels without continuously feeding them. It is a toy in two parts - one stick with a peanut attached to a string, and one with a large green hoop.

The currency set for this item meant that the borrower of the Squirrel Fun Toy had to prove that a squirrel had jumped through the hoop.

Tomek and Marlon O'Connor testing the first Squirrel prototype on the Flower Walk.

" The Squirrel Fun Toy created an interactive space in the park, between the park users and the squirrels, and between the people who run the park and its visitors. The ring, the Squirrel Fun Park, was an actual space in itself, a space for interaction."

Tomek Rygalik, Product Designer, former RCA student
Meeting at the RCA, 23/01/2006

36

From: Tomas Klassnik, Date: Mon, 16 Aug 2004 18:55:40
To: PARKPRODUCTS@SERPENTINGEGALLERY.ORG
Subject: squirrel safari

Alex Goforth and Tomas Klassnik got a squirrel to pass through a designated hoop at 5.40pm on Sunday 15/08/2004.

Please find attached some JPEG images documenting our successful attempt to get the squirrel through the hoop [more a tentative step than a jump].

If possible I would like to be kept informed about any similar projects in the future, as I enjoyed this activity very much.

Yours,
Tomas

(10 out of 90 people who tried the toy suceeded)

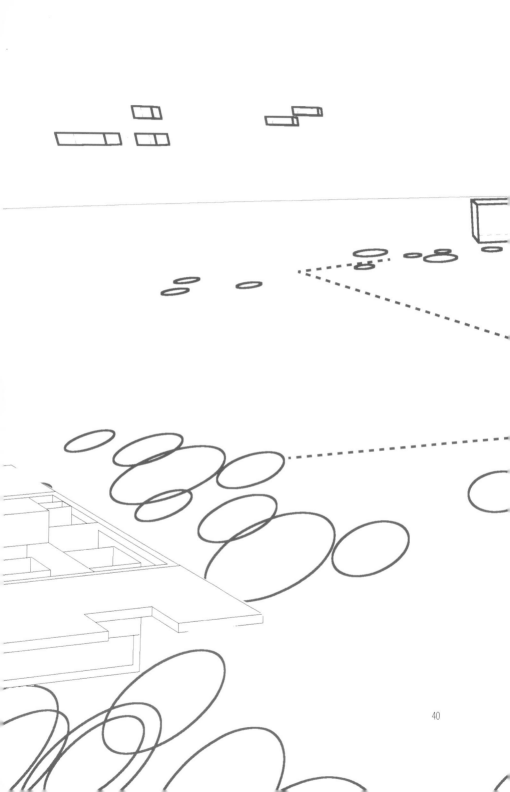

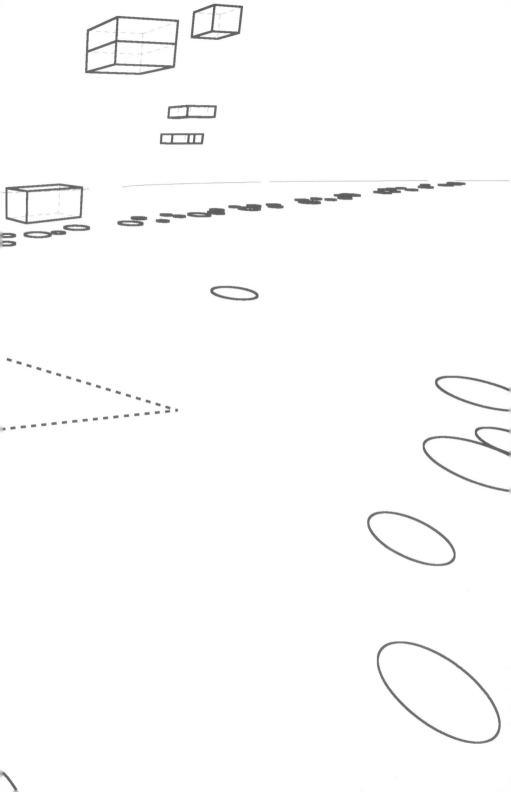

Serpentine Gallery

Spaces used throughout the project.

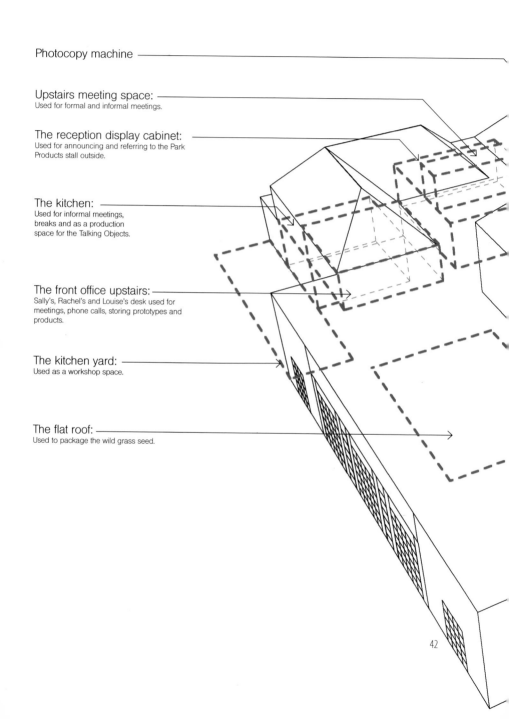

Photocopy machine

Upstairs meeting space:
Used for formal and informal meetings.

The reception display cabinet:
Used for announcing and referring to the Park
Products stall outside.

The kitchen:
Used for informal meetings,
breaks and as a production
space for the Talking Objects.

The front office upstairs:
Sally's, Rachel's and Louise's desk used for
meetings, phone calls, storing prototypes and
products.

The kitchen yard:
Used as a workshop space.

The flat roof:
Used to package the wild grass seed.

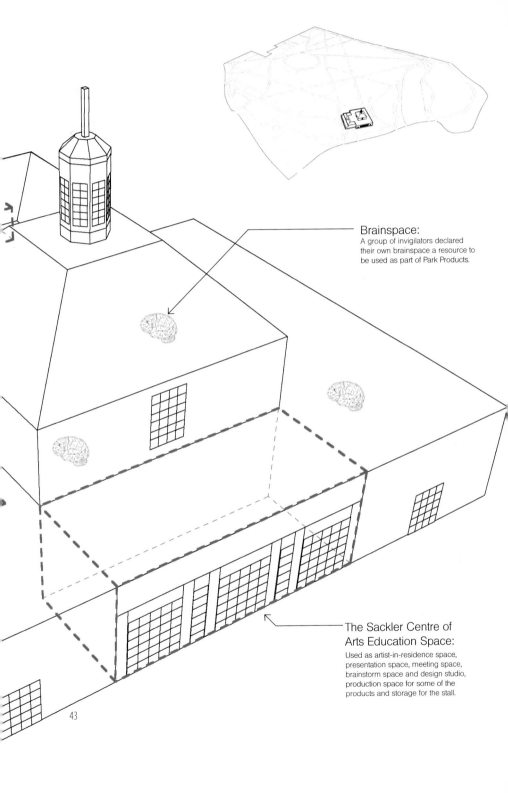

Brainspace:
A group of invigilators declared
their own brainspace a resource to
be used as part of Park Products.

**The Sackler Centre of
Arts Education Space:**
Used as artist-in-residence space,
presentation space, meeting space,
brainstorm space and design studio,
production space for some of the
products and storage for the stall.

43

Local institutions

Local institutions formed part of a network of resources for Park Products and extended the geographical and physical space of the project in terms of meeting and production spaces, as well as allowing for a local social and creative space to emerge.

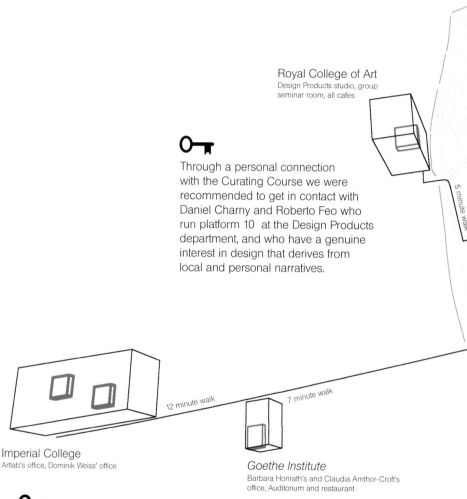

Royal College of Art
Design Products studio, group
seminar room, all cafes

Through a personal connection with the Curating Course we were recommended to get in contact with Daniel Charny and Roberto Feo who run platform 10 at the Design Products department, and who have a genuine interest in design that derives from local and personal narratives.

5 minute walk

12 minute walk

7 minute walk

Imperial College
Artlab's office, Dominik Weiss' office

Goethe Institute
Barbara Honrath's and Claudia Amthor-Croft's
office, Auditorium and restaurant

It turns out that Bennie Connolly, the head of the groundwork team in Kensington Gardens, plays in a band with Dominik Weiss, who is a Geochemist at the Imperial College. He gets involved with the Invisible Cards product, where water and water quality becomes an important aspect.

44

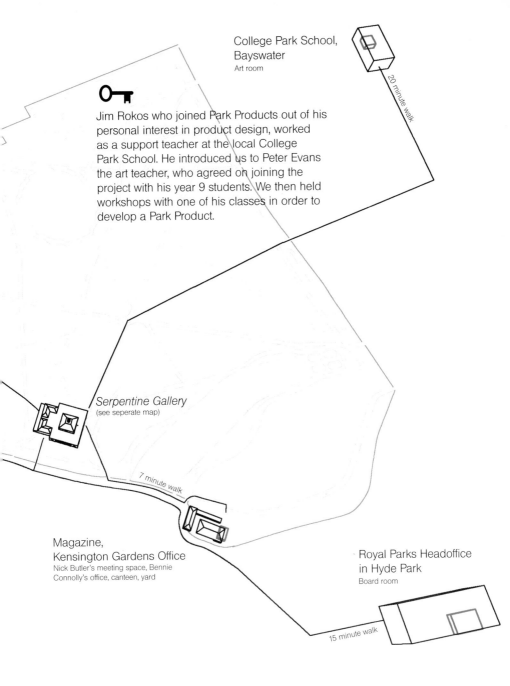

College Park School,
Bayswater
Art room

20 minute walk

Jim Rokos who joined Park Products out of his
personal interest in product design, worked
as a support teacher at the local College
Park School. He introduced us to Peter Evans
the art teacher, who agreed on joining the
project with his year 9 students. We then held
workshops with one of his classes in order to
develop a Park Product.

Serpentine Gallery
(see seperate map)

7 minute walk

Magazine,
Kensington Gardens Office
Nick Butler's meeting space, Bennie
Connolly's office, canteen, yard

Royal Parks Headoffice
in Hyde Park
Board room

15 minute walk

45

Frieze Art Fair, Regent's Park ——— 20 min van ride →
Auditorium

Viewing platform

20/01/2004

A visit from the Kensington Palace gardeners group to the Royal College of Art, to see the design and production facilities available at the Design Products studio.
On the way back down from the 7th floor the view over their work place, Kensington Gardens came as a surprise.

Kensington Palace garden

Royal College of Art

Links across

We met Harry Crystal, a part-time gardener in Kensington Gardens, who showed us around the material yard on a Saturday.
The previous year he had found a camera in one of the park bins and kept it to take photographs of the park. We met in his flat in Shoreditch to go through the photographs and talk about the idea of developing a Park Product based on his images and observations.
We never finalised the product, though he later applied successfully for an arts grant from the Royal Borough of Kensington and Chelsea, using the link to Park Products.

Flat in Shoreditch

Bin

Leaf Yard

Production spaces

All products make use of the existing resources of the park and its immediate neighbourhood, its natural, cultural and social resources.

The production space for each product includes
- the area from where the narratives and material are sourced
- the rooms used for design workshops
- the facilities where the prototypes and products were made.

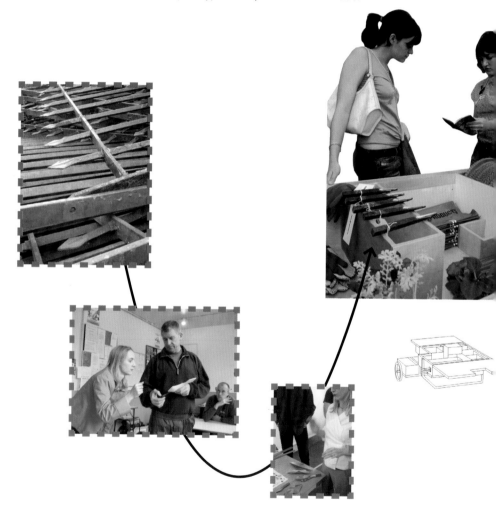

The Fence Tool makes use of the disused green iron railings that are distinctive to the park, and stored away in the Leaf Yard. The idea and the prototype were developed through workshops and presentations both at the gardeners' canteen and the Royal College of Art design studios.

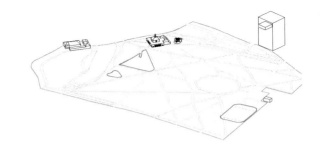

Large parts of the grass area in Kensington Gardens is left uncut during the summer months to provide a natural habitat for wildlife, and to protect the ground soil from drying out. The fine fescue grass plant is indigenous to Kensington Gardens. The grass seed is harvested and cultivated for use in the park, and some of the 2004 harvest was packaged for Park Products.

The idea for the Magpie Charms comes from sightings of magpies in the western part of Kensington Gardens. The magpie jewellery was developed between Angelika Seeschaaf and the Kensington Palace gardeners group, using their small hut near Kensington Palace and the metal workshop at the Royal College of Art.

Overnight production

The Chompost Bar is a compressed bar of compost formed into the shape of a chocolate bar, meant as a special treat for your plants at home.

It uses organic Royal Parks compost from the park. Each autumn, the leaves from all Royal Parks across London are collected and piled into a huge fuming and smelling mound in the Leaf Yard at Kensington Gardens.

For the Chompost Bar the compost is collected from the Leaf Yard, driven over to the Magazine Yard where the bars were produced by pressing compost into custom-made moulds.

The filled mould was left overnight under the hydraulic legs of one of the heavyweight vehicles used by the gardeners.

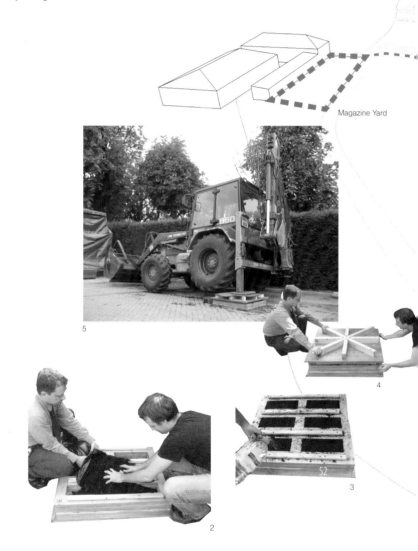

Magazine Yard

5

4

3

2

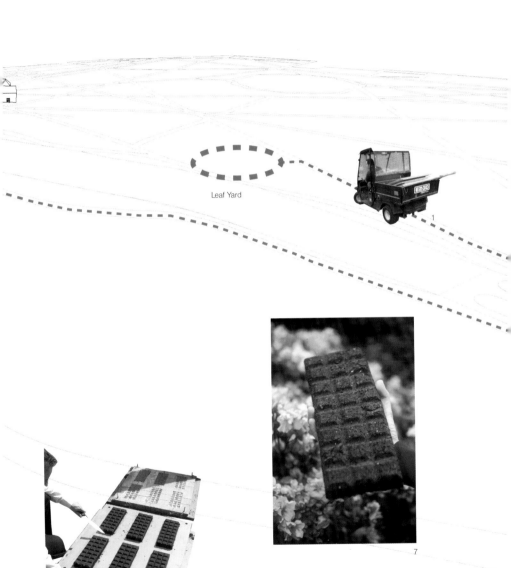

Leaf Yard

1

7

53

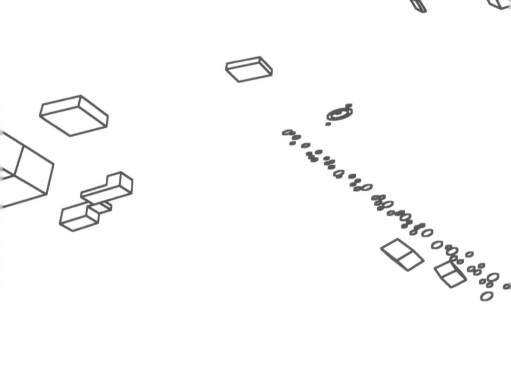

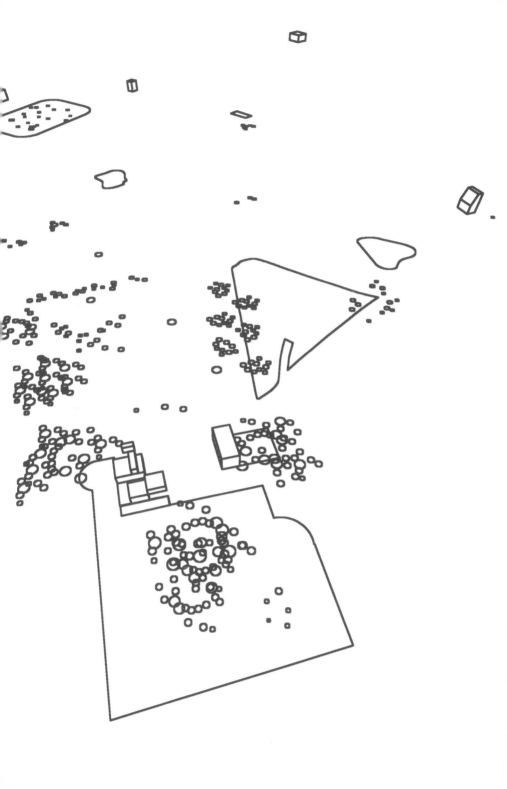

Brain space

One of the available resources which was quickly identified by the Serpentine Gallery Assistants, was their own brain space, which they felt was heavily underused during their long hours of invigilation.
They're not supposed to do anything obviously distractive during their working hours in the gallery.

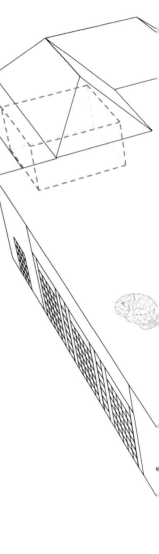

Brain space could be used invisibly and the gallery assistants started to invent narratives for found objects from the park, which were often left at the reception desk at the Serpentine.

The short narratives were recorded on a small device during their tea and lunch breaks in the staff kitchen.
The found object were placed on the recording and playing device would then go on the Park Products stall.

The Talking Objects were exchanged for similar found objects.

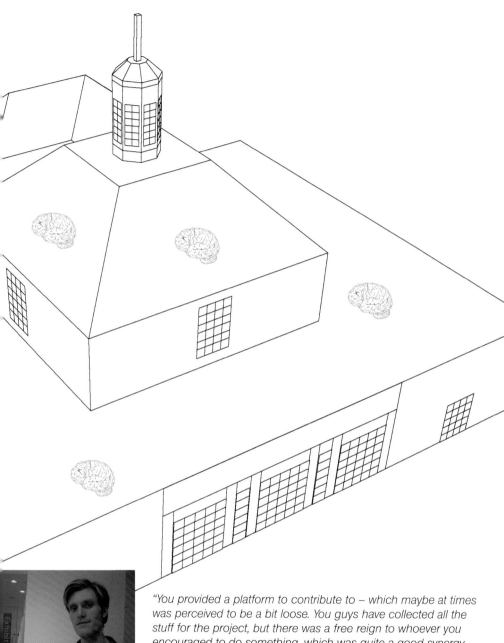

"You provided a platform to contribute to – which maybe at times was perceived to be a bit loose. You guys have collected all the stuff for the project, but there was a free reign to whoever you encouraged to do something, which was quite a good synergy. There was an encouraging feel to the whole project.

Park Products encouraged a different mind set. It was a creative reaction to the surroundings and the stall was the hub where it all came together.

The best thing about it was that it occupied a space in your mind, it was good here (he said hitting his chest)."

istian Glaeser, artist and gallery assistant
eting in the reception of the Serpentine
lery, 20/01/2006

Space of conflict

Park Products proposes a model for cultural production and distribution which questions familiar relationships and rules, i.e. the designers become collaborators with members of the public and the trade is based on a non-monetary currency. The whole project evolved through an ongoing process of negotiations, both formal and informal, light-hearted and aggressive talks.

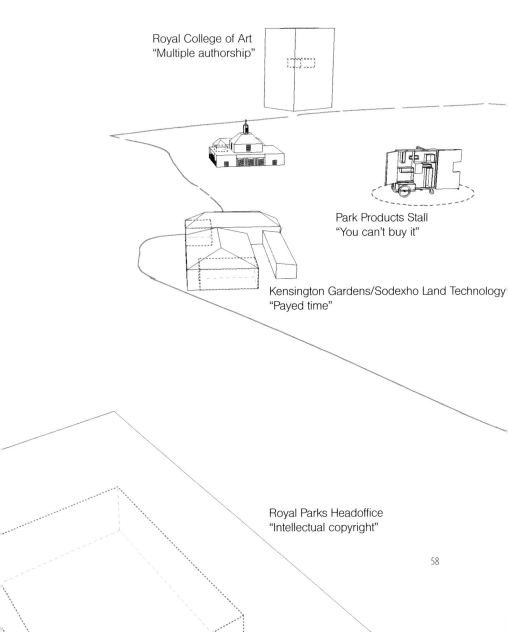

Royal College of Art
"Multiple authorship"

Park Products Stall
"You can't buy it"

Kensington Gardens/Sodexho Land Technology
"Payed time"

Royal Parks Headoffice
"Intellectual copyright"

Sally Tallant, Head of Education and Public Programmes, Serpentine Gallery
Upstairs meeting space at the Serpentine, 30/01/2006

" The moments of conflict and the conflicting objectives of different parties involved in the project were interesting points where the project was negotiated. You, the Serpentine, all of the institutions, the individuals, everyone involved in the project had different viewpoints and expectations.

The project manifest itself through negotiating these conflicts, whether they were small or large, like for instance the discussion of copyright.

Every project requires negotiation, but you as the artists decided to share authorship and copyright in this project, which puts negotiation at its heart."

Summer pavilion

The annual Serpentine Summer Pavilion is sited on the lawn in front of the Serpentine Gallery. In 2004 the proposed Summer Pavilion by MVRDV Architects had been rescheduled and the lawn remained empty. The Launch of Park Products and the market stall took place on the site of the Summer Pavilion on 28th July 2004.

The launch marked the end of the Product Development Phase which had involved a number of participant groups and the beginning of the Trading Phase with the general public of the park.

Park Products is a social space based on the principles of informal exchange. The intention and infrastructure of the project allowed for new social encounters between very different individuals and groups. The project generated a space that could be experienced through encounters but didn't manifest itself as a built structure.

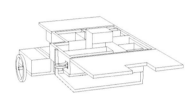

On the day of the launch the Park Products market stall was used in it's horizontal position as a trading table.

60

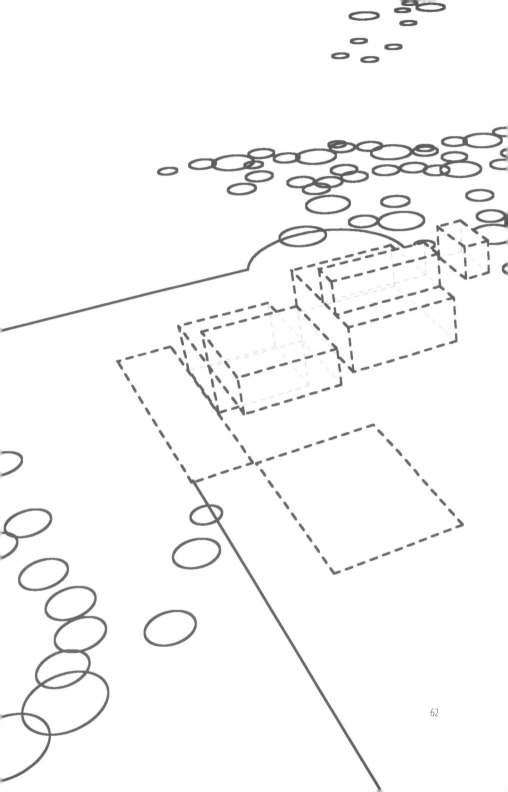

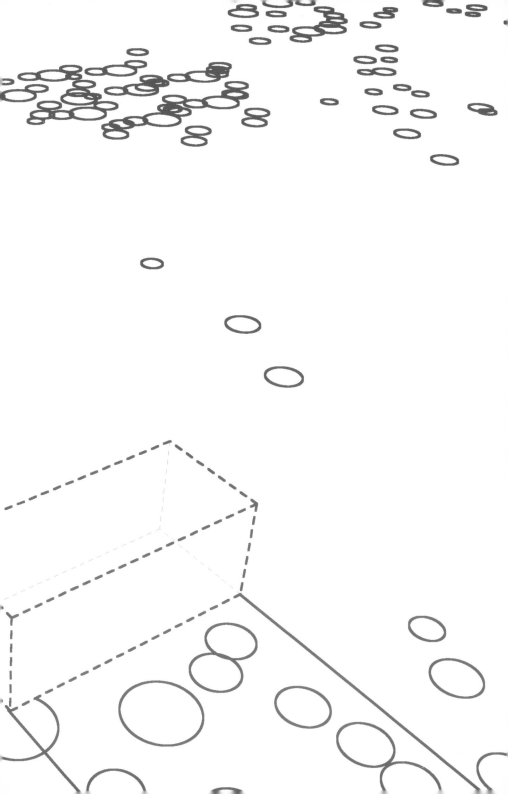

Compost heap

The final manifestation of Park Products is not predictable in advance and depends entirely on the actions of the users of the Park. If we consider the aesthetic qualities of the work through the practices of production and consumption initiated by the various users, as makers and exchangers, how important then are the artist and architect's conceptualisations of these relationships?

I asked Böhm and Lang if they had choreographed Park Products, pre-selected the user groups and instigated certain rules of conduct, or had they let things emerge more organically? Böhm and Lang were emphatic – it was the latter. This made me reconsider my own position. Rather than press forward to try to uncover the processes that I felt sure had been used conceptually to structure the project, I realised the situation asked for a different approach. To choose to relinquish control over the final work, and hand the decision-making process over to others, asks for a new form of critical engagement – not a holding down, but a letting go.

Extract from Dr Jane Rendell's essay "Letting Go" for the Park Products Brochure,
Published by Serpentine Gallery and Kathrin Böhm and Andreas Lang, 2004*

Julia Peyton-Jones, Director, Serpentine Gallery
Mobile phone conversation, 02/02/2006

"You asked me, if I think of Park Products as a space, which space comes to mind? I think of it as a compost heap, because it has to do with the exterior and the interior having such different qualities. The exterior is sculptural and highly textured. The interior is degradable and a synergy of things. A compost heap is like a volcano, it brings energy through and the heat of the inside juxtaposes the cold air outside."

* The Park Product brochure can be downloaded as a pdf file from
www.publicworksgroup.net

Market place

The Park Products stall had daily opening hours from 2.00pm to 6.00pm, accompanied by one or two stall guards, who would explain the barter based trade to visitors who wanted to get one of the items. The currency for each product was set by the same group who developed the product.

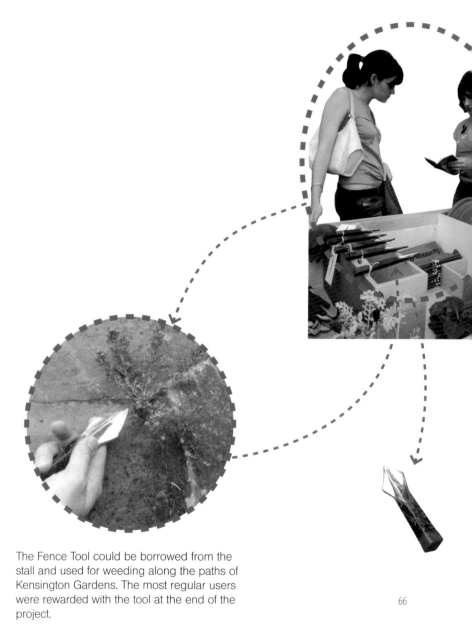

The Fence Tool could be borrowed from the stall and used for weeding along the paths of Kensington Gardens. The most regular users were rewarded with the tool at the end of the project.

66

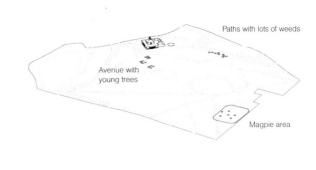

Paths with lots of weeds

Avenue with
young trees

Magpie area

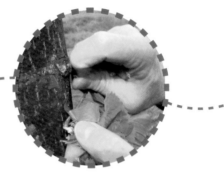

In exchange for the Wild Grass Seed from
Kensington Gardens visitors were asked to
help with one vital element of park maintenance.
They were asked to carefully rub down the growth
sprouts on young tree trunks along one of the
paths near the Serpentine Gallery, in order for the
trees to grow tall and straight.

A certain area in Kensington Gardens provides
home for numerous pairs of magpies. The Magpie
Charms refer to the superstitions associated with
magpies, especially their love for shiny objects.
Magpie Charms were to be left in a tree in the park,
with a wish scratched into their soft silver surface.

All around access

"The Park Products stall functioned as a very accessible space. It could be seen and accessed from all directions of the Park, and the different sites of the stall itself allowed different access. People could come from behind and just have a look through the display window. They could stop by and listen to the conversation that was going on at the stall, while someone else could come straight up to us for a chat. The stall was quite self-explanatory in itself. It also generated a mix of very different people."

Polly Brannan, artist., one of the stall guards on site
Meeting at public work's office on Tuesday, 23/01/2006

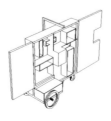
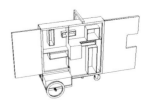

Meeting space

While visiting Jim at his studio at college he introduces us to his course leader who happened to have seen Park Products in action.

Ben Hughes, Course Leader Product Design, Central St. Martin College of Art & Design
Chance encounter, 24/01/2006

"The best thing that I remember was the guy looking after the stall. He was the guard who drew us in, that is my most enduring memory, this slightly strange guy, hanging out there, and we just stumbled over the stall, but he got us involved and got us to do all those things. I did the water thing, the Tray for Two, and offered a drink of water to a woman in the park. She really wanted to know if it was mineral water and where it came from. The water turned out to be from Fiji. We got talking and it turns out that she was a dealer in Chinese antiques. I had just inherited some Chinese antiques and we stayed in contact. Later she came to my house to explain the different pieces to me, and estimated their value. It all developed into a kind of friendship."

The Tray for Two was developed together with Laurent Trenga, the Catering Concessions Manag for the Royal Parks. In order to get the tray, one ha to offer a drink of water to a stranger in the park a start a conversation.

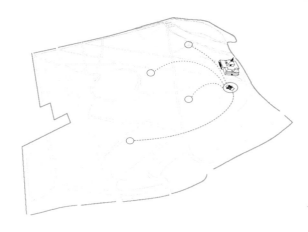

7/09/2004
The Water Experiment.
his was an interesting social phenomena. Much
ss about offering water than about intervening
someone else's space. I approached a man
nd his daughter (I'm also a man). The man really
lt intruded upon, and was not receptive at all,
uite suspicious, and not at all warm. He did take
drink, though his daughter did not, and she
idn't smile until I fetched a balloon and made his
aughter an adorable teddy bear (my own trick!).
knew this would finally break the ice, though
e remained rather bothered with the whole
xperience."

14/08/2004
"I approached a lady on her way to the
Serpentine Gallery and offered her water.
She gratefully accepted as it was a hot day.
She looked very young but said she was
52…! This gives me some hope for my
future. Well, I am 33 but she thought I was 27.
Thanks for the opportunity for a friendly chat
with a stranger. And thanks for the day."

24/09/2004
"Offered a glass of water to a woman
walking a dog. She wasn't thirsty but
liked the smily face tray. She told us
that her dog had heard a strange noise
and when she turned around she saw
a pair of wild parrots flying together.
Apparently they are the descendants
of some parrots who escaped several
years ago and mated."

Roaming extension

The mobile Park Products stall was the physical hub and interface of the project, where the different groups and audiences met. During August and September 2004 the stall was out in Kensington Gardens on a daily basis and open to the public between 2.00 pm and 6.00 pm.

The stall physically extends the action radius of the Serpentine Gallery Programme into the public realm of the park and becomes a roaming spatial extension for the institution.

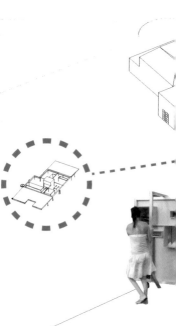

Louise Coysh, Project organiser, Serpentine Gallery
Meeting at one of the coffee huts in Hyde Park, 20/01/2006

"Park Products was an extension of the gallery, the public would stumble across the stall in the park, and different levels of conversation and engagement took place.

The project, with its non-monetary economy, subverted consumer/viewer expectations. The structure of the project was an exchange of conversations amongst otherwise unconnected individuals, with a language that evolved as the project progressed. For many park users the mobile stall created a bridge into the gallery.

Park Products highlighted the Serpentine Gallery's interest in challenging the contexts where art practice exists and can be experienced.

Your ambition with Park Products was never the gallery space, it was clearly the public realm and the park."

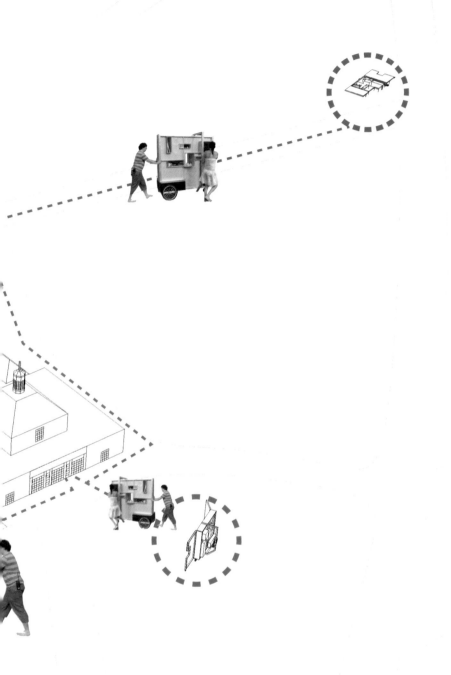

Polly:
"I think the stall could have moved further away from the gallery, but there were limitations, because we were on our own and had to be able to go to the toilet, or bring the stall back in quickly when it rained. There were a number of health and safety reasons why we had to stay in close distance."

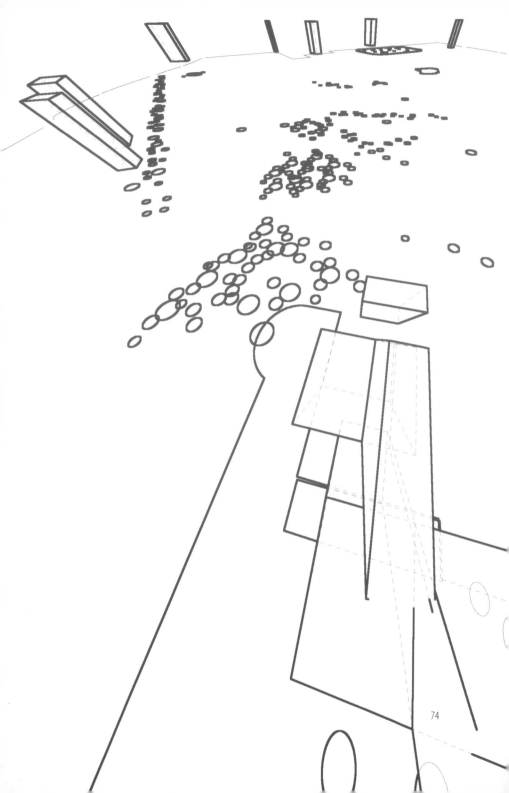

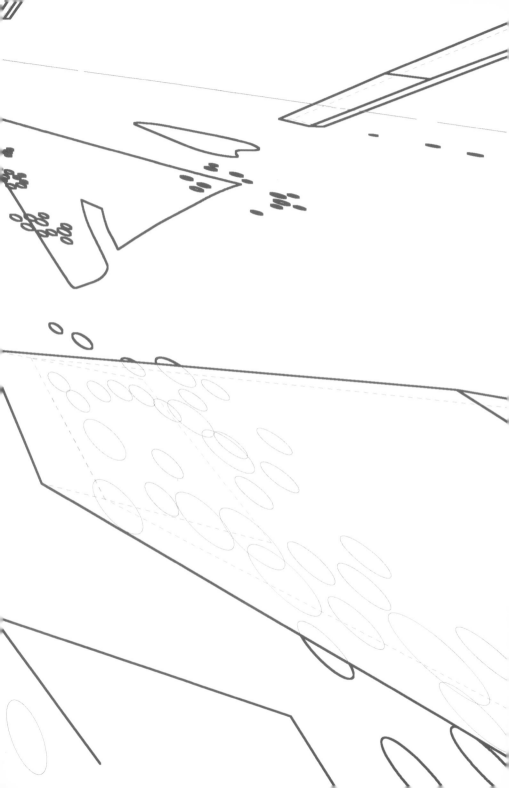

Working with uncertainty towards a real public space

Doina Petrescu

'Brocante' (car boot sale) organised by local residents involved in the ECOBOX project, Paris, La Chapelle, May 2004

Working with uncertainty towards a real public space

community to come

The challenge of this article is to show—to stir thinking in a more creative and politically open way—the relationships between institutional bodies, formalised structures and more fragile, informal agencies, including small groups and individuals, in the process of transforming communities and places.

The term 'community', is at the core of all regeneration programmes, and remains for me problematic when used uncritically, and tokenistically, as in the language of governmental policies and regeneration programmes. In this discourse, 'community' is a generic term undifferentiated and associated with deprived neighbourhoods. It is, as Jeremy Till puts it in our co-edited book *Architecture and Participation* '*a wishful and wistful hope that fractured territories can be reconsolidated into some semblance of community, without ever specifying what that word may actually mean*.'[1] As such, 'Community' is a 'C' in a combined abbreviation: NDC (New Deal For Communities), ACU (Active Community Unit), CEF (Community Empowerment Fund) etc., that express government ambition to '*tackle the problems of deprived neighbourhoods*' and provide subsequent financial support.

I would like to start by taking the term 'community' out of its abbreviated meaning and its association with poor neighbourhoods and governmental care, in order to bring it into a more critical perspective. Additionally, I would like to introduce a contemporary deconstruction of this term, which informs the dominant Western political formation, founded upon totalising, exclusionary myths of unity and setting at the core of our modern thinking of *the social*.

Artists, philosophers and political theorists have critically approached the notion of community, trying to understand the sense of 'being-in-common' beyond the generic and undifferentiated term. They have looked outside the restrictive meanings relating to exclusive communities, or as identity-oriented communities that recognize themselves only through common rules or unifying characteristics; whether language, race or religion. They have introduced a notion of community that exists only through time and space determinates, in the very articulation of person-to-person, of being-to-being, in all that constitutes the living world, forming the idea that a *community* is related to a specific time-space-location; suggesting that the politics of community cannot be separated from the politics of place. The

Community cannot be conceived other than in the process of becoming; a continually receding horizon of a 'community to come', which will never be reached, but must constantly be worked towards.[2]

Questions around the term 'community' in socio-politics, overlap with those surrounding the notion 'public' in art and architecture. Like 'community', 'public' is a generic notion, most often understood as what is 'common', of shared or of common interest, or as what is accessible to everyone. 'Public' has a cognitive dimension, but also a political and poetic one. It may also have a double meaning, of social totality and specific audiences. The notion of 'public' has been variously articulated, ie. 'public realm', 'public sphere' or 'public space'; each time conveying an ambiguity and multiplicity of meanings.

Many architects and planners today advocate the necessity of having more public space in the city. In *Towards an Urban Renaissance*, the final report of the Urban Task Force in 1999, Richard Rogers calls for such public spaces, envisaging them as squares, piazzas, unproblematically open to all. However, as Doreen Massey notes in her recent book *For Space*, '*from the greatest public square to the smallest public park, these places are a product of, and internally dislocated by, heterogeneous and sometimes conflicting social identities/relations*'.[3] This is what gives *real public dimension*. **Public space** should be, then, described in terms of its evolving relations, as *a space in permanent mobility*, not only *physical* but also *social* and *political*. Architects and urban planners might learn that creativity is required where the conflicting nature of public space is revealed; by way of imagining solutions, or of making sense together, etc.

On this point, contemporary art practices are maybe advanced. Rather than the centralised and fixed notion of 'public', inherited from modern theories, many contemporary artists, curators and cultural workers have started to address the public within its *fluid* and *plural* forms; speaking about 'publics' constructed as '*elusive forms of social groupings articulated reflexively around specific discourses*'.[4]

As Jorge Ribalta puts it, '*the public is constructed in open, unpredictable ways in the very process of the production of discourse and through its different means and modes of circulation. Therefore, the public is not simply there, waiting passively for the arrival of cultural commodities; it is constituted within the process itself of being called. The public is a provisional construction in permanent mobility.*'[5]

The type of practices that operate in the public realm, their discourses and their tools, are strategically very important, as they are always formative; potentially constructing the public and making the community.

multiple and informally produced public space

Making community and making space for community cannot be separated. Planners and architects might start to consider the inherent social and relational dimension of the spaces they create, and to integrate their specific temporalities and mobilities into the design process. The Lefebvrian understanding of the 'production of space' being social and political is now widely accepted, far beyond Marxism and sociology, as a base for any sustainable approach in urban development. The question that remains is that of methodology and critical innovation, the degree of openness of the different professional and political frameworks that commission such approaches, which might leave room for unpredictability and bottom-up proposals issued from real claims. The architectural production of public space could start by identifying the claims for it. Sometimes these claims are modest and informal, but what is important is how to transform them into a brief, a challenge, and sometimes a proposal that will give room to the multiplicity of desires and needs of diverse sets of users.

An example is given by art and architecture group *muf*'s project *Small Open Spaces that are not Parks*, commissioned by the Stratford Development Partnership, on behalf of the London Borough of Newham, in 2003. This was a commission to work with residents to identify small open spaces suitable for investment, devising programmes and identifying sources of funding for them, and acknowledging the need to make provision for young people in the borough. Through extensive consultation, thirty four sites have been identified across the borough, including unexpected types of **open spaces**, that people felt were 'public' including *a pedestrian bridge, a cinema foyer, underpasses, a strip of pavement outside a chip shop, an alleyway bridge, a cinema foyer and an alley frequented by girls only*. *muf* translated this street expertise into a brief and a proposal, which stated a typology of spaces that considered all the recorded claims. They concluded by building one of these typologies, a 'social cage'; a roofed sports area designed as both spatial and sporty. What is important is the multiplicity and smallness of these proposals, which express the scale of use, the modesty but also the precision of claims.

dealing with the messy, complex, lives of users

There is a 'non-planning' tradition in British architecture which starts in the 1970s: an architecture represented by practitioners like Cedric Price and theorists like Rayner Banham, Peter Barker and Peter Hall, who aimed at subverting the planning legislation and 'putting planning back into politics' by promoting freedom, social mobility and participation[7]. From that architecture, still believing in the modernist values and the revolutionary role of technology, practices like *muf* and **public works** have kept their resistance to imposed aesthetics, their playfulness and enthusiastic attempt to get people to shape their own environment.

The important drive for participation that was originated by critical practices in the 1970s, has now became the Government's mantra. In the UK and most European countries, urban policies and regeneration practices encourage 'community participation', but by lacking specificity they generate stereotypical approaches and reiterate fixed notions of 'community' and 'public space'. The existing frameworks of both governmental and local participative programmes are organised in the same way, without taking into account the particularity of each situation. Participation becomes an organised (and potentially manipulated) part of any regeneration project, in which the users are meant to be given a voice, but the process itself erases the outcomes. The problem is also that the term 'participation' is accepted uncritically, idealised and centred on concepts of consensus [8]. This is what some would call a 'pseudo-participation' and, as Till suggests, the question for contemporary architects and planners would be *'how to move from it to a transformative participation, how to suggest a positive transformation of architectural production that benefits architects and users alike'* [9]. This transformative participation *'makes confrontation with difference inevitable, as the users will bring to the table their personal beliefs. In the negotiation of the personal with the social, the individual with the collective, political space emerges'.* This is something that architects, who are still obsessed with maintaining control over space through their buildings, could learn; that art practices can provide tools and critical methods to approach what goes beyond strict management, to reveal the political nature of space. Artists are also sometimes better positioned to deal with the 'messy, complex, lives of users'.

'stealth architecture'

The contemporary art theorist and curator Stephen Wright has remarked on the emergence in the past few years of a broad range of practices that can be described as 'art-related' rather than 'art-specific' activities.[10] They constitute a kind of 'stealth art', operating in contexts often far removed from art-specific spaces and infiltrating spheres of 'world-making' beyond the scope of work operating under the banner of art. They are considering art in terms of its specific means, its tools and its competence, rather than its specific ends as artworks. Within these practices, *art remains free to deploy all its symbolic force in lending enhanced visibility and legibility to social processes of all kinds*. Art perceived as a 'latent activity' has another function, or in Wright's terms, a 'use value': *it crops up in the everyday not to aestheticise it, but to inform it*.

In questioning the role of architectural practices in revalidating everyday life activities and giving back value to existent places, maybe a 'stealth architecture' could also exist: an architecture which would deal with architecture-related activities, rather than architecture-specific ones; which would consider architecture in terms of its specific means (tools, competences, processes), rather than its specific ends (constructions and buildings). What would it be, this architecture which 'crops up in the everyday' not to give it a form, but to inform it?

This is a question that I have also raised in my own practice, as a member of *Atelier d'Architecture Autogérée* (AAA), a collective practice including architects, artists, urban planners, landscape designers, sociologists, students and residents living in La Chapelle area of Paris. Together we conduct research into participatory urban actions. This practice allows for the re-appropriation and reinvention of public space through everyday life activities (gardening, cooking, chatting, reading, debating, etc.), understood as creative practices in urban contexts. The aim is to create a network of self-managed places by encouraging residents to gain access to their neighbourhood and to appropriate and transform temporary available and under-used spaces. It is an approach that valorises a flexible and reversible use of space, and aims to preserve urban 'biodiversity' by providing for a wide range of life styles and living practices to coexist. The starting point was the realisation of a temporary garden, made out of recycled materials on one of the derelict sites belonging to the RFF (the French Railway company), located in the area. This garden, called **ECObox**, has been progressively extended into a platform for urban creativity, curated by the AAA members, residents and external collaborators, catalysing activities at the level of the whole neighbourhood. It literally has cropped up in the neighbourhood's everyday life. [11]

What is interesting for all the practices mentioned above, is that none are described as architectural in a traditional way. These practices are located 'in-between', and their proposed devices are meant to increase this 'be-tweeness'; to reveal what is different but also what is common within a multi-angled approach, by sharing methods and inventing cross tools. This sharing of methodology and hybridisation increase creativity and open up unexpected possibilities of thinking and acting in the public realm.

tactical approaches of public space

In *The Practice of Every Day Life*, Michel De Certeau analysed popular culture not as a 'domain of texts or artefacts but rather as a set of practices or operations performed on textual or text like structures'.[12] He shifted the emphasis from representations in their own right to the 'uses' of representations. In other words, how do we as consumers use the texts and artefacts that surround us? And the answer, he suggested, was 'tactically'. He described the process of consumption as a set of tactics by which the 'weak' make use of the 'strong'. He characterized the rebellious user (a term he preferred to consumer) as tactical, and the presumptuous producer (in which he included authors, educators, curators and businessmen) as strategic.

The question poised of all strategic policies, is how to address this rebellious user, how not to discipline or erase him or her, how not to exclude informal dynamics, but how to integrate them with their own role? The tactical dimension involved in, say, **public works'** practice covers aspects of information and communication. The types of connections are diverse, varying from random encounters or informal and opportunistic associations, to reciprocal interests and shared affinities. A practice that tactically creates relationships and ways of exchange between a broad set of social actors, between different 'worlds' is also a political practice. *'Politics are not made by power relationships but by relations between worlds',* says Jacques Rancière[13]. Practices like those of **public works** are innovative not only in bringing new skills and tools, but also new conceptions of 'the public' as relational, articulated and communicated in architecture. By encouraging crossover and mixing between urban programmes, institutional frameworks, art events, educational contexts and everyday life, such activities locate the public in the

conflictual and divided, in the fragmented and permissive, in different spaces
of experience and the peculiarities of existence.

the peculiarities of existence

Katherine Shonfield stated in her article written for the 2002 Urban Summit,
that the role of art practices in regeneration contexts exists precisely to seize
these peculiarities of existence and
allow ordinary people to feel more
empowered. *'In the confrontation of
the fragility of the individual with the
robustness of policy, much of the peculiarities of existence, which form a large
chunk of the subject and form of art, are
filtered out. Hence, paradoxically, it is
policy, which is sometimes a less than
real view of the everyday world that urban regeneration directly addresses. Art
is special in that it can both sustain and
contain these peculiarities; for art there
is no particular point to be proved, no
constituency to be won over. For art, the
success of an endeavour can be the net
effect of recognition and acknowledgement of peculiarity. For strangely, such
acknowledgement makes people in general feel a lot less peculiar and therefore,
a lot more empowered'.* [14]

This idea—of making the users feel
more empowered in their confron-
tations with rules and policies—is
what Shonfield identifies as the role
of art in urban regeneration. Could this not become, by extension, the role
of an architectural practice as well, if this practice accepts getting rid of its
authority and power, and starts to 'sustain and contain' the peculiarities of
existence? AAA defined itself as a practice which enables inhabitants to participate directly, to decide how they want to organise themselves, knowing
that sometimes the community desires could be different from the public
or private interests. Both residents and professionals become equal members in a 'bricolaged' structure: *'what happens depends upon what people bring*

with them and what they do once they are there'. This kind of structure also preserves a certain economic and political independence in the negotiation process with both private and public bodies. But at the same time, it is a structure which takes risks, because nothing can be taken for granted when everything depends on the presence of all those involved. Sometimes this presence is conflictual, for people's desire change along the way, and one

should learn how to deal with tensions, contradictions, oppositions and failures. The residents also participate in the invention of new tools for multiple and flexible use. For example, a series of modules of mobile furniture have been co-produced by AAA members, eco-designers, residents and students, to function as urban catalysts and mobile extensions of the ECObox garden: these include an urban kitchen, a 'bibliomobil', a media lab, a rainwater-collector and a joinery workshop. They generate infrastructure and networks, stimulate desire and pleasure at the scale of proximity. Inhabitants can use them for different activities to appropriate space within the city. Nobody is in control of the outcomes of these practices: neither the architects, nor the institutional representatives, not even the community.

This lack of power is at the same time an enormous power. It is not the power of making things for the community, of representing it, (which is the architects, planners and regeneration officers' privilege), but of participating in making the community itself, through discrete spatial interventions. It is a performative shared experience of community: 'community is coming about, or rather, is happening to us in common', as Jean-Luc Nancy says [15].

public space of proximity

A renewed approach to architecture and urban planning cannot be initiated solely by centralised structures and governmental bodies. It must also include 'microscopic attempts' at the level of collective and individual desires within the micro-social segments of public space: neighbourhood associations, informal teams, self-managed organisations, small institutions, alternative spaces and individuals themselves. Urban development policies need to learn how to make provision for such attempts.

The micro-dimension of **public works'** interventions (i.e. manufactured objects, improvised urban furniture, cleaning and gleaning, etc.), bring precision, detail and localisation with the public space. These activities are additionally effective in their attempts to change and transform space. The scale of proximity, the small scale devices and the walking distances that demarcate the area of intervention, bring another quality to the networks and the relationships between participants. They increase intensity of living.

As with AAA's project in Paris, and *muf's* project *Small open spaces that are not parks*, small scale can come to define the public space itself. Such projects are based on the temporary appropriation and use of leftover spaces and urban interstices, and commonly include waste space from the real-estate market, or due to the temporary neglect of the urban planning policies. These are 'other spaces', the 'other' to what constitutes the 'planned' city. Studies have demonstrated that in big cities they function as an alternative to conventional forms of public space, that nowadays are more and more subject to surveillance and control. The 'leftovers' are spaces of relative freedom, where rules and codes can still be redefined. These 'spaces of uncertainty', to borrow Kenny Cupers and Markus Miessen's term [16], are the very opposite of the functional spaces of the city, and recast public space as heterogeneous, fragile, indefinite, fragmented and multiple. The status of these spaces inspired AAA's strategy, the aim of which was to leave space for 'others', others than the usual actors of the urban planning process, visible and less visible users, through a process that would enable them to get involved in the decision making and take control over spaces in the area where they live. It is also a political process. The problem is how to avoid freezing functions in these spaces, while conserving their flexibility, their programmatic 'uncertainty', their fragility and indefiniteness.

Another way to create a public space of proximity is through sizing temporary dynamics. The AAA strategy tries to manage these different temporalities, politics of use, and ownership statuses to propose, instead, temporary inhabitations that will create new usages and new urban functions in the area. Temporality supposes mobility and multiplicity. The mobile furniture modules, acting as urban catalysts in the area, generate temporary agencies, and form progressive networks of actors. As the aims are continually evolving according to new spatial opportunities, participation becomes a process-in-progress. Usually, the participative process is solidified as soon as the goals are met: when a contested space is occupied, a project is built, etc. The role of these temporary agencies and emerging networks is to keep the use of space and the process of decision open.

The sustainability of such processes within temporary (architectural and art) interventions, might be one of the concerns of regeneration programmes. Formalised regeneration commonly initiates systematic interventions without considering the dynamics that precede them. Allowing (both in terms of funding and politics) spaces to function with their own dynamics, encouraging different temporary and self-managed agencies to emerge in time would be a solution to stir public participation and make it a sustainable and transformative process.

This is how a real public space should be: *'A symbolic, identitary and complex territory, where the social sphere overlaps with the political, cultural and economic sphere. A space in which these elements are newly composed again and again within diverse and fragile communities in permanent dialectic with an increasingly global society. A public space of proximity is, in other words, where the discourse on the collective good is rooted in everyday social practices, in a common material space with its multifaceted meanings'.*[17]

How to make sense together through a design process is, as noticed by Till, the question of any (architectural) practice which operates *in a social world where meaning, though often multiple, ambiguous and conflicting, is nevertheless a perpetual practical accomplishment*.[18]

In my article *Losing control, keeping desire*,[19] I have stated the necessity for

architects to take another position, which releases the illusion of being in control of their architecture and gets closer to the users' positions. Rather than being a master, the architect should understand himself/herself as one of the 'participants', and work with meaning as a perpetual practical accomplishment. Till considers that in current participative practice, *architects tend to cling to the certainty of what they know rather than expose themselves to the uncertainty of what others may know*.[20] The uncertainty of what 'others' may know (may desire, may live, etc.), is something which critical practices might need to impress upon their colleagues—architects and planners. I would include in these 'others', all kinds of users; but also all kinds of clients, officers and commissioners; indeed, all kinds of collaborators. Clients and commissioners, regeneration officers and neighbourhood managers might also gain by opening up their programmes, policies and structures to this uncertainty; as a condition for increased creativity and critique within regeneration programmes and community participation.

References

1. J. Till, 'The Negociation of Hope', *Architecture and Participation*, P.B Jones, D. Petrescu, Jeremy Till (eds), Spon Press, London 2005, p.23

2. 'Philosophical inquiries into the notion of the community' by Jean-Luc Nancy (*The Inoperative Community*, 1983), Maurice Blanchot (*The Unavowable Community*, 1983) and Giorgio Agamben (*The Coming Community*, 1993), seek to open it up toward a broader politico-ethical context. Nancy's call for the deconstruction of the immanent community has been particularly influential: community as the dominant Western political formation, founded upon a totalizing, exclusionary myth of national unity, must be tirelessly 'unworked' in order to accommodate more inclusive and fluid forms of dwelling together in the world, of being-in-common.

3. D. Massey, *For Space*, Sage Publications, London, 2005, p 152.

4. M. Warner, *Publics and Counterpublics*, Zone Books, New York, 2002.

5. J. Ribalta, 'Mediation and Construction of Publics : The MACBA Experience', http://republicart.net/disc/institution/ribalta01_en.htm

6. muf is an all women art-architecture practice

7. See J. Hughes and S. Sadler (eds), *Non-Plan Essays on Freedom, Participation and Change in Modern Architecture and Urbanism*, Architectural Press, Oxford, 2000, pp. 2-22.

8. For example *Architecture and Participation* criticises pre-formatted participative approaches and suggests innovative approaches, which are both creative and critical.

9. J. Till, op. cit., p.31.

10. S. Wright, 'The Future of the Reciprocal Readymade: An Essay on Use-Value and Art-Related Practice', www.turbulence.org/blog/archives/000906.html

11. *Atelier d'Architecture Autogérée*, founded in 2001, in Paris, operates now as a translocal network (www.urbantactics.org). For more details see my article ' Losing control, keeping desire', *Architecture and Participation*, pp. 43-64.

12. M. de Certeau, *The Practice of Everyday Life*, University of California Press, Berkley, 1984.

13. J. Ranciere, *Disagreement: politics and philosophy*, University of Minnesota Press, Mineapolis, 1999

14. K. Shonfield, 'We need artists' ways of doing things - A critical analysis of the role of the artist in regeneration practice', *Architecture and Participation*, p. 225.

15. J-L. Nancy, *The Inoperative Community*, University of Minnesota Press, Mineapolis, 1991

16. K.Cupers and M.Miessen, *Spaces of Uncertainty*, Wuppertal, Verlag Müller, 2002

17. A. Membretti, 'Centro Sociale Leoncavallo: The Social Construction of a Public Space of Proximity', www.republicart.net

18. J. Till, op. cit. p. 33.

19. D. Petrescu, 'Losing control, keeping desire', *Architecture and Participation*, p. 56 and passim.

20. J. Till, op. cit. p. 31.

Series Editor and Production: Anna Douglas.

Commissioning Editors: John Butler, Anna Douglas, Janet Hodgson.

Artist project: public works.

First published in Great Britain in 2006 by Article Press, in association with ixia.

Copyright © Article Press/ixia 2006.

Artist project copyright © public works.

Essay text copyright © Doina Petrescu.

Interview text copyright © John Butler and Janet Hodgson.

Photographs: public works and David Bebber.

Graphics: public works and Sara de Bondt.

Every effort has been made to trace the copyright holders, but if any have been overlooked the publishers will be pleased to make the necessary arrangements at the first opportunity.

With thanks to Emma Larkinson for initiating the series, on behalf of ixia.

All opinions expressed within this publication are those of the authors and are not necessarily those of the publishers.

John Butler is an artist/curator and Professor of Fine Art at the Birmingham Institute of Art and Design, a Faculty of the University of Central England.

Janet Hodgson is an artist and a senior lecturer in Fine Art at the University of Central England.

public works is a London based Art/Architecture collective who use physical and conceptual frameworks to address the relationship between formal and informal social structures.

Design by Gérard Mermoz @ Semiographics.

Printed by Warwick Printing Ltd, Leamington Spa.

ixia PA Ltd, 1st floor, 321 Bradford Street, Birmingham, B5 6ET, www.publicart-thinktank.org
Article Press, University of Central England, Margaret Street, Birmingham, B3 3BX.
t. 0121 331 5970, articlepress@uce.ac.uk
Distributed by Central Books, 99 Wallis Road, London, E9 5LN.
t. 0845 458 9916.
orders@centralbooks.com

This publication is supported by:

PROJECT
engaging
artists
in the
built
environment

Artists' acknowledgements:

Serpentine Gallery

With special thanks to Sally Tallant and Louise Coysh, Julia Peyton-Jones, Sara de Bondt, Nick Butler from the
Royal Parks, Bennie Connolly of Sodexho Land Technology, Christian Glaeser, Tomek Rygalik, Lynn KIngelin,
James Rokos, Sew Lang Nielsen, Marlon O'Connor, Polly Brannan, Ben Hughes, Lawrence Barth.

Kathrin Böhm is supported by:

 Arts & Humanities
Research Council

Colophon

Cover
set in *Myriad Pro* regular and semibold.

Title page
set in *Myriad Pro* light, semibold and italic.

Foreword
set in *Myriad Pro* light condensed, light condensed italic and condensed italic.

Section headings
set in *Myriad Pro* light, regular, italic semibold, and condensed.

Interview
set in *Myriad Pro* condensed, condensed italic, light, light italic, and italic.

Project
set in *Helvetica BQ* light and light italic (set by public works).

Essay
set in *Adobe Jenson Pro* regular, italic, semibold and semibold italic.

Credit page
set in *Adobe Jenson Pro* condensed.

Typography and graphic design by Gérard Mermoz @ Semiographics.
t 024 76 405 772 . mob. 07817 289 451 . gerardmermoz@hotmail.com

Printed by Warwick Printing Ltd, Leamington Spa, UK.
t 01926 883 355 . www.warwickprinting.co.uk